A Psychologist Prescribes

for emotional and relational problems

Dr. Sandeep Atre

INDIA · SINGAPORE · MALAYSIA

ISBN
Paperback 979-8-89744-614-8
Hardcase 979-8-89906-253-7

Contents

Introduction

Yes, I know that the psychologists do not write prescriptions. They work with their clients' thoughts, emotions and feelings to bring required changes in their behaviors, actions and choices. But if they could, what would they prescribe for emotional and relational problems? Well, in my work as a Counseling Psychologist, I have come to realize that, in addition to the personalized therapy a client goes through, a lasting change requires development of new skills.

So, I believe that, if a psychologist could prescribe, they would prescribe what I call 'skill-pills' - intake of a skill-development pursuit to supplement therapy or counseling. In this book, I have selected ten such skills that together cover most of the skill-requirements to aid successful solutions for intrapersonal and interpersonal issues. I envision a psychologist (or a person on his or her own) picking one of the skills from this set and visualizing it as a pill.

I have chosen an unusual format for this book. I write about each skill in terms of "what it is about", "what are its ingredients" (written in form of an acronym, so that it is easy to remember) and "why and how its ingredients work" (explaining each element of the acronym in details). I have made sure that, for each of the headings or sub-headings, I write only three paragraphs, so that you find it an easy read. After all, it is easier to take smaller pills.

Dr. Sandeep Atre

1

Dis | Tol

The 'Distress Tolerance' Skill-Pill

What is it about?

Simply stated, distress is 'bad stress'. You may ask "Is there something called good stress?" Yes there is. It is called Eustress. While eustress is the optimum amount of stress that helps a person to reach the sweet-spot of stimulation and performance, distress is the level of stress that affects all faculties of a person adversely. Interestingly, while the triggers of distress are different for each one of us, the symptoms are typically the same.

In distress, irritability increases and one feels a force rising inside the body that is highly eager to get out of one's system in any form – raising voice, expressing nonverbally, aggressing physically, or withdrawing entirely. Well, we all get distressed at some point in time, but we all differ in our ability to tolerate distress; due to factors ranging from genetic, developmental to social. Having said that, here we are concerned with, not the state, but the episode of distress.

In such an episode, something triggers us and all of a sudden one gets absolutely overwhelmed by what is going on inside. For people with low distress-tolerance, these episodes are quite hard to handle. The bottom-up impulse to react is so overpowering that the thinking centers of the brain get shut down, and people end up behaving in a way that runs the risk of sabotaging their well-being, relationships and goals. A potent prevention to this is the skill-pill – **DisTol**.

What are its ingredients?

BREADS they are:

B – Breathe deeply

R – Rejig physically

E – Evacuate immediately

A – Act oppositely

D – Divert multi-sensorily

S – Self-talk chantingly

Why and how do its ingredients work?

Breathe deeply:

We all know why we breathe – to take in oxygen and expel carbon dioxide with the help of lungs. It's the all-important function of body that keeps us alive, that's why it's an automatic one. However, the Autonomic Nervous System (ANS) of one's body keeps shifting the breathing rate to accommodate one's need of oxygen. For instance, when our brain is preparing our body to fight or flee, the oxygen needed will be more and thus our breathing rate changes.

Same happens in case of distress. In a way, distress is a modern variant of primitive 'fight or flight' case, so the breathing pattern changes when one is experiencing it. Typically a distressed person begins to take small and shallow breaths, using their shoulders. This superficial over-breathing (called hyperventilation) creates a loop of sorts that only worsens the state as, while the feeling of distress causes such breathing, such breathing in turn causes feeling of distress.

The solution is 'deep breathing' – technically speaking the 'diaphragmatic breathing' (also called belly breathing). Diaphragm is a sheet of muscle underneath the lungs. When one breathes deeply involving diaphragm (often called 4-7-8 breathing, i.e. breathing in for 4 seconds, holding the breath for 7 seconds, and exhaling for 8 seconds), the 'rest and digest' mode of one's ANS gets activated, thus there is normalization of heart-rate, perspiration and salivation.

Rejig physically:

In a way, emotion can be seen as 'energy in motion' or 'energy mobilization'. When people feel any emotion, invariably, there is a physiological reaction. When people don't get to make larger moves like fleeing or fighting, they would still fidget, touch, fiddle, hold, play, fold, shake, clasp, pat, clench and what not! If seen from another angle, these actions are helping energy to come out of one's system, as energy can neither be created nor destroyed but only change forms.

Let's not forget that that's precisely what distress is targeting. It has suddenly created a scenario of thrust in energy that is warranting some sort of action. The last thing you can do now is to not do anything, as it is theoretically almost impossible. In fact, the more you are suppressing the external action, stronger the internal movement of energy is. That results into an increase in urge that, after every attempt to control, keeps coming back more vehemently.

So get into any movement within the range of permissibility and properness that can release the building-up energy inside your body – adjust yourself in the chair, change your posture, move facial muscles, stretch your arm or leg muscles, play with something around you, get up and start pacing to and fro, grab a stress ball, move fingers or hands rhythmically, tap a surface repeatedly, pat or hit one hand with other in a restrained way. So, whatever it is, make a move.

Evacuate immediately:

When you are in distress, all the variables of the situation – person, place, presence of other people, nature of the apparatus, tempo of the conversation, heat of the moment etc. – are now involved in priming you towards letting off the steam. The combined effect of all of it makes it harder for you to fight the urge to react. That's why, in spite of knowing what to not do, people are compelled to do exactly that – all under the influence of the confluence of these variables.

That's why it is important to get away from the situation so that one can first of all be relieved of the pressure that various variables of the situation are exerting subliminally on them. This can come in the form of excusing oneself from the place temporarily on some pretext (a bio-break is often a good choice, and so is the need to make a phone call) or even formally proposing a hiatus to gather the thoughts and de-clutter the mind.

In the worst-case scenario, it should be okay to simply walk away just like that (you can always make up an almost plausible reason on your way back) if you feel that asking for permission can elicit a reaction that might trigger you more. It is important to get oneself ejected entirely and not play in the head what had just happened. This timely act of plugging oneself out from the sensory interlock and subsequent decrease in sensory load helps you cope with the situation.

Act oppositely:

William James, who is often called the father of American psychology, profoundly said that *"Action seems to follow feeling, but really action and feeling go together; and by regulating the action, which is under the more direct control of the will, we can indirectly regulate the feeling, which is not"*.

It gives us a tip to deal with distress. After all, when one is already chaotic inside, rather than trying to whisper wisely amid shrieking sentiments, it's better to work outside-in.

It is almost on the lines of what we learnt in Physics – to break the state of inertia, apply an external force. Even Marsha Linehan, the creator of famous DBT (Dialectical Behavior Therapy) confirms this approach when she says *"When one acts in the ways that are opposite to what one is feeling, the feedback to the brain does not confirm the emotion. Consequently one may not only ease the emotion, but even change the way one is feeling"*. Pretty much in line!

Even CBT (Cognitive Behavioral Therapy) confirms this. One of CBT's key tenets is that our emotional experience has three components – thoughts, feelings and actions. And each can change the other two. So, for instance, if you are angry, act (verbally and nonverbally) as if you are calm – slow your gestures down, take up an unaggressive posture, break eye contact or stare laterally in a defocused manner, speak with pauses and lower the pitch of voice. It works.

Divert multi-sensorily:

In some ways, emotions are like a water stream. If it is coming at you with full force, rather than trying to stop it head-on, it is better to redirect it. Similarly, when an emotion is in full swing, it is better to change it than to control it. Tony Robbins gives a hint on how to do it when he says "Where your attention goes, your energy flows". So when you divert your attention, you also divert the emotion (as we discussed earlier, emotion can be understood as 'energy in motion').

How can attention be diverted? Well, the best way to do it is by changing our sensory inputs. After all, our five senses are the doors to our consciousness and cognition. So whenever you are in distress, quickly take new sensory input that can divert your attention. It is always better if you make this diversion a multi-sensorial one. Why depend on one sense? Flood the sensory channels with new information that flushes out the stuff that is forming distress response.

So sip some tea (water of course is better, because it will also improve hydration, which is one of the three major metabolic fuels for the brain), eat a candy, go to restroom and splash some water on your face (if it is a little cold then even better), inhale something (a new or unusual fragrance will work even better), wash your eyes gently, listen to a song or a tune, watch a quick clip, observe surroundings, read a quote, or feel wind on the face. The More the better!

Self-talk chantingly:

Chanting, in simple terms, is repeatedly uttering the words of significance. You must have seen people carrying a 'thread of beads' across almost all the religions. They typically count beads while chanting silently or whisperingly. It is a powerful ritual for calming the 'monkey mind', bringing attention inwards and keeping one's wisdom stable. In moments of distress, we can't take out beads, yet for tolerating distress better, we can apply one part of the ritual – chanting.

Research studies have shown a strong connection of chanting with changing neurochemistry (for instance, a boost in the production of Nitric Oxide that helps regulate the nervous, immune and cardiovascular systems, which in turn can help increase blood flow and muscle relaxation). Chanting has also been found to have a role in the activation of Vagus nerve, whose stimulation can improve vagal nerve tone and one's ability to intentionally counteract the distress signals.

You can choose a mantra, a couplet, a prayer, an affirmation, a quotation, or a message to self. It can be a quote (like "This too shall pass" or "I am not my thoughts" or "One day at a time" or "Do not take it personally"), a Sanskrit mantra, a Buddhist chant, a Bhagvad Geeta verse, a line from the Lord's Prayer, or an Ayat/Ayah. Now, begin to say it repeatedly to yourself in your head. It will help you log out of chaos, bring your attention inward, and calm yourself down.

2

The 'Emotional Regulation' Skill-Pill

What is it about?

Emotional regulation is one of the core therapeutic skills to learn for those who struggle with behavioral and relational problems. It is the ability to start, stop or steer one's emotional state and its manifestation in a way that is aligned with a constructive goal. It involves a continuous process of tracking the ongoing and ever-changing demands of the situation, monitoring one's emotions, evaluating suitability of emotions in context of demands, and then adapting aptly.

Emotional dysregulation hurts on interpersonal as well as intrapersonal fronts. Interpersonally, it poses difficulty in developing and maintaining healthy and synergistic relationships in both personal and professional spaces. On intrapersonal front, it leads to oversensitivity, meltdowns, tantrums, and even self-sabotaging behaviors. What's worse is that people with dysregulation are often branded as unstable, temperamental, childish, immature and even crackpots.

While struggling with emotional dysregulation, some people opt for unhealthy strategies like withdrawing from active engagement with people, indulging in excessive social media usage, abusing alcohol or other substances, and even harming oneself. Even from a situational point of view, people grappling with dysregulation tend to either internalize or externalize emotions, each of which has destructive side effects. A potent prevention to this is the skill-pill – **EmoReg**.

What are its ingredients?

EVENTS they are:

Stay aware of:

E – Extrapolation of cause-effect chain

V – Vulnerability hotspots

E – Emotional profile

N – Nervous-system signals

T – Tendency for lateral movement in discussions

S – Subliminal factors

Why and how do its ingredients work?

Staying aware of:

<u>E</u>xtrapolation of cause-effect chain:

Extrapolation is the process of using existing information to predict what is likely to happen in future. When a person is struggling with emotional dysregulation, first to get compromised is the ability to envision how their current action will impact all the stakeholders. This inability to imagine things across the coordinates of time and space leaves a person blind towards the cascading chain of 'cause and effect', as one thing is bound to lead to another and so forth.

Let's take an example. Suppose you see your kid doing something that you find really irritating, and you feel a strong urge to shout at her. But currently there are people around you. Now, if you shout at her in front of people then she will not only feel bad but also embarrassed. This episode can impact her ability to interact socially, her ability to trust you with her secrets, her willingness to take you along in her circle, or her faith in your ability to protect and guide.

Now you may think that that's the whole point! If the ability to extrapolate is compromised then how can we apply it? Well, the good news is that the sheer (and mere) willingness to think holistically and futuristically (even a thinking pause) brings thinking centers of the brain online, and with initial difficulty, process of "getting back to one's senses" begins (howsoever feebly). Now it's just a matter of allocating cognitive bandwidth. Hereon, what you feed shall prevail.

Vulnerability hotspots:

People become more susceptible to emotional dysregulation when some intervening factors are at work. Some of them are common to us (of course to a varying degree) and some unique to each of us. Let's take common factors. Two prominent ones are tiredness and hunger. In both, people's reservoir of will-power (thus self-control) is depleted. It makes them more reactive than they realize or imagine (ever heard the term hangry – hungry + angry).

Another factor is lack of sleep. Sleep is to brain what coolant is to a car engine. With insufficient sleep, people become grumpy or foggy. With continued sleep-deprivation even of a few days, one is prone to poor behavioral control, lousy decision-making and a tendency to spot and spread negativity. Same happens when someone is unwell. Threshold of touchiness becomes low and people lose control on smallest of things, and that too in an eruptive manner.

Then there are personal factors – Some people hate Mondays, some have aversion to early mornings, some don't like high temperatures, some dislike cloudy days, some get triggered by closed spaces, some get upset when they are hurried into a work, some are irritated by noise, some get repelled by casual approach of people. Whatever this factor is, it is important to be aware of this vulnerability hotspot and mindfully deal with it or work your way around it.

Emotional profile:

One's emotional profile can be seen in terms of four major parameters – speed, intensity, duration and frequency.

Speed can be seen as "how quickly does a person get emotional". Intensity can be seen as "how strongly does a person feel the emotion". Duration can be seen as "for how long does a person keep feeling the episodic emotion". Frequency can be seen as "how often does a person get emotional during a certain timeframe".

One's emotional profile is a product of multiple factors like upbringing and experiences, and there is a definite genetic component to it, because of which, one's emotional profile remains relatively permanent. While it is desirable to challenge this notion, it is also wise to be aware of one's emotional profile and utilize this awareness to make apt adjustments and choices. Working with emotional profile is a complex matrix yet even a one-dimensional effort pays off.

For instance, if speed is high then the person can learn to read the early cues of a building emotion; If intensity is high then the person can learn to express emotions without getting emotional, so that the steam is let off in installments; if duration is high then the person can learn the deliberate skill of self-disclosure; and if frequency is high then the person can learn the formal structured way of catharsis that will prevent the accumulation of emotional debris.

Nervous-system signals:

Every emotion has a corresponding physical manifestation. These physiological markers of emotions are regulated automatically 'beneath our conscious control' by our Autonomic Nervous System (ANS). ANS makes our internal organs work according to the emotional state being felt. Now, there are two discrete types of emotional states – tense and relaxed. Tense state is often called 'Flight or Fight' and relaxed is often called 'Rest and Digest'.

In tense state, ANS gets activated in what is called Sympathetic mode. For instance, in fear, pupils dilate to bring in more light to be able to observe as much as possible, respiratory rate increases because your body needs more oxygenation for energy and stamina, heart rate increases because more blood-flow is required throughout your body and glucose-release increases through liver as now body needs sugar for energy.

On the other hand, in relaxed state, ANS gets activated in Parasympathetic mode, and all the aforementioned markers get normalized. Well, keeping track of what your body is saying to you gives you 'Self awareness' – an essential quality of a sorted person. With it, you can decide upon the most apt response in a situation. Moreover, what better, you can also see how well that response worked, on the basis of the change in autonomic signals given by your body.

Tendency for lateral movement in discussions:

There is a strange tendency I have observed in people who struggle with emotional regulation. They tend to go 'back and forth' and sideways in discussions. They find it nearly impossible to stay on course during a conversation. They fetch old grudges, recall unrelated incidents, quote something from past entirely out of place, change topic to accommodate a whim that emerged in their head, or pick any secondary or tertiary thought-thread to sabotage the primary one.

Why do they do so? They are simply drunk heavily on emotions and are obsessed with keeping an interaction emotionally charged and sentimentally stimulating. Energy in their bodily system intends to spill itself out and wreak havoc. Their rationality takes a backseat and objective of the conversation zeroes in on a metaphoric fist fight. This personal idiosyncrasy often seduces the other person into behaving likewise and then the discussion reaches a point of no return.

So whenever you are part of a discussion, create in your head a sentinel – a conscience keeper, a tail twister, a watchdog. Their job is to see if what you are speaking is in line with the topic and objective of the discussion. Do not get derailed. Stay on course. Whenever you feel a desire to quote something which is not contextually relevant then check what is leading to this intention. More often than not, you will find a subliminal factor (discussed next) at the root.

<u>S</u>ubliminal factors:

Subliminal refers to something that is operating below the level of consciousness but has an influence. While we all would like to believe that our actions and reactions are commensurate, logical and regulated, it remains a fact that we are largely governed by the factors we are not consciously aware of yet are strongly driven by. Staying cognizant of their intervening role can help us prevent emotional dysregulation better, or revert to baseline sooner.

For simplification, let's see them as ABCs. In any situation, firstly it is important to be aware of our own assumptions, apprehensions and aspirations; i.e. it is vital to confirm our notions, not let our concerns affect our judgment, and guard our perspective from our agenda in a situation. Secondly, it is vital to be aware of our background, biases and back-stories; i.e. filter the effect of where we are coming from, what we hold a thing against and what has led to where we are.

Thirdly, it helps to be aware of our complexes, comparisons and constraints; i.e. neutralize the impact of what we don't like about ourselves vis-à-vis others, what we benchmark ourselves against, and what our limitations in terms of resources are. Needless to say, if we can also be aware of other people's ABCs then it works even better. In all, the idea is to step aside and see if our choices and decisions are heavily loaded with the emotional baggage accrued elsewhere.

3

The 'Interpersonal Connection' Skill-Pill

What is it about?

We aren't called social animals for nothing. We are wired to connect. In fact, we are so hungry for connecting that we tend to build associations with everything around us —spaces, devices, possessions, plants, animals, birds, and of course, fellow human beings. These connections are at the heart of our well-being in every sense. While connecting with people should come most easily to us, a counterintuitive fact is that that's precisely where our biggest problems emerge.

For most people, it is easy to connect with everything but humans, probably because there is a scope for exercising a one-sided control. In case of human connection, there is more ambiguity, complexity and variability. Even in the most rigidly formed systems of human interconnection with clear standard operating procedures and defined code of conduct, there will always be an element of unpredictability. It's because there is no readymade solution to manmade problems.

In absence of an algorithm, all bids of interpersonal connections are fraught with some amount of stress. As a result, people either try to avoid connecting or fail in connecting well. In either case, consequences are huge. All mental and emotional problems have an interpersonal angle to them. Whether it is depression, anxiety, disillusionment, stress or conflict, the deficit of healthy interpersonal connection plays a part. A potent prevention to this is the skill-pill – **IntCon**.

What are its ingredients?

LEVER they are:

L – Listen without distraction or restlessness

E – Enter other person's psychological mind-space

V – Validate other's feelings by feeding back

E – Express your perspective as hypotheses

R – Remain open to the 'back and forth' process

Why and how do its ingredients work?

Listen without distraction or restlessness:

Why do we get distracted? Actually, our brains have ability to think a lot faster than someone can speak, and that extra capacity leads us to distraction. The point is beautifully captured by author Kate Murphy and Ralph Nichols (often called the father of listening research). Murphy talks about a term 'Speech-Thought Differential'. A person typically speaks at a rate of about 120-150 words per minute, which takes up only a small portion of our thinking bandwidth.

As a result, listener wanders in their excess cognitive capacity. As Nichols masterly put it – *"To be a good listener means using your available bandwidth not to take mental side-trips, but to double-down on your efforts to understand and intuit what someone is saying"*. In other words, the desire for stimulation, externally (people and devices) or internally (thinking and imagining), has to be checked. The act of active listening helps in this – best captured by acronym LISTEN.

Listening can be seen as the acts of Looking, Indenting, Smiling, Tilting, Expressing, and Nodding. Maintaining a humble eye-contact activates our mirror neuron systems, which makes it easier to empathize; verbal indenting (words like "I understand") helps in creating a feedback loop; smiling (only if context allows) helps in building rapport; tilting conveys interestedness; apt facial expressions build trust; and nodding indicates that you are sincerely receptive.

<u>Enter other person's psychological mind-space:</u>

A well-known term for this would be 'empathy'. However, empathy is of two types – emotional empathy and cognitive empathy. When we are totally present in the moment where the interaction is occurring and listen through our ears as well as eyes then, by virtue of our mirror neurons, we simulate or represent the emotional experience of the other person inside ourselves and know firsthand what it feels like. This vicarious act brings emotional empathy.

In cognitive empathy, a different concept is at work. It is called the 'theory of mind'. It is the ability to explain and predict other person's behaviors by utilizing the shared world knowledge, linguistic structures and social cues. It is fundamentally different from emotional empathy in the sense that while emotional empathy is rooted in the feeling of oneness, ToM begins with the very acknowledgement of the fact that the other person is separate from you and different.

So we apply our knowledge of other person's beliefs, circumstances, desires, fears etc. to undertake an automatic inferential process leading to cognitive empathy. Thus, emotional empathy is about how other person must be feeling and cognitive empathy is about what other person must be thinking. Together, they offer integrated view to a person's psychological mind-space. Having said that, it starts with genuine desire and sincere effort to understand someone.

Validate other's feelings by feeding back:

Validating someone's feelings doesn't necessarily mean that you are agreeing or consenting, it means that you understand their feelings. It shows that you can see from their point of view and know how it looks like from there. It shows respect and helps in establishing trust, as the other person feels you both are on the same page. It proves that you are not dismissive of their stand, and find it legitimate, regardless of whether or not it aligns with your views on the issue.

Sentences like "I can see you are deeply hurt", "It must be hard for you", "I can only imagine how you must have felt" or "I can sense it is not at all easy" go a long way in making the other person feel validated. However, the key is to not just say these words but to also mean them, as an insincere effort to validate is akin to manipulation. Moreover, it is important to let validation sink in before you start to solve the problem or resolve issues. Don't hurry into the next steps.

Emotional validation is a great tool for defusing intense emotions. It instantaneously helps the other person to get over the feeling of "Me vs. them"; because, in one's heart, no one likes to be misunderstood, misinterpreted or misrepresented. That's why it helps to repeat, replay, rephrase, recapitulate or reflect the other person's feelings in their own words, metaphors and syntaxes. It makes them feel reassured that nothing is lost in translation or transaction.

Express your perspective as hypotheses:

It is people's rigidity that makes connecting so complex. In the name of clarity and surety, we often express our opinions in a manner that rubs people the wrong way. Theodore Roosevelt (or John Maxwell) put it beautifully – "People don't care how much you know until they know how much you care". When we come across as arrogant or abrasive then people get defensive and even discount the due merit of our point. There's just too much heat to bear or ignore.

A good way to prevent this problem is to express perspective, not as gospel truth or a fact, but as a hypothesis. It is a profound term that means "a logical idea that is suggested as a possible explanation for something yet is open to verification through deliberation, experimentation and study". Delving into the term's research roots, it can also be seen as "a clear testable statement that guides the direction and focus of discussion, while still being falsifiable and revisable".

In other words, when you say sentences starting with "According to me…", "In my view", "As per data…", "On the basis of…" or "My initial feeling is…" then you are telling that what you are saying is based on observation or grounded in theory but isn't something on which you have shut yourself off from reasoning or analysis. You can even declare at the outset that you are proposing a hypothesis and are open to discussion. It sets just the right tone for the interaction.

Remain open to the 'back and forth' process:

Hurry to reach conclusions or agreements is one of the biggest mistakes one can commit in the realm of interpersonal connection. Often people feel that it is absolutely futile to stay in long winding conversations as it is a sheer waste of time. While it is true if this becomes a repeated pattern, the 'back and forth' exchanges are a way for people to subconsciously collect valuable information about each other's styles, preferences, likes, dislikes, triggers and thresholds.

This information (which can be called 'small data') helps them to connect with each other in a much deeper manner, and to subtly adjust their own ways of communicating, coordinating and cooperating. This customization is at the heart of interpersonal connection, as this is what translates into what is often called 'rapport'. It lays the foundation for future interactions that get navigated so intuitively that there is an effortless flow, giving a sense of mutual fulfillment.

So whenever you wish to connect with someone in a meaningful way, keep patience for the organic process of consolidation to run its due course. It will happen brick by brick and you have to pour the cement of 'respect irrespective of agreement'. It's only when people disagree without being disagreeable, challenge without being aggressive, confront without being rude, and debate without being derogatory that interpersonal connection brews gradually but solidly.

4

The 'Clear Communication' Skill-Pill

What is it about?

Communication plays the all-important role of 'lubricant' in the interpersonal machinery of our social world. They are right when the say that "You cannot not communicate". Even silence is a form of communication. That's why it is better to get it right, because if you don't get it right, a lot goes wrong. It becomes even more important in relationships that are newly formed, going through a change, emotionally charged, strategically important or unusually sensitive.

In each of these cases, clarity of communication becomes 'make or break' factor. Interestingly, most people only realize it after the damage is already done. Look around! There is no dearth of evidence of it. Dig into any story of dysfunctional family, broken relationship, sour partnership or struggling friendship and, more often than not, at the root, you will find a lot of trust-deficit caused by missing, improper, untimely, distorted, ambiguous or violent communication.

In this context, psychologist Marshall Rosenberg came up with an important term – nonviolent communication. Though what he says under the term was said by people before him, none said it better (in fact what you are going to read in the next section owes a lot to four components of nonviolent communication). In all, the loss and failure of communication is a major cause of interpersonal issues and challenges. A potent prevention to this is the skill-pill – **CleCom**.

What are its ingredients?

SEAM they are:

S – Share observations without sounding judgmental

E – Express feelings without tagging the other person

A – Assert your needs without sounding demanding

M – Make clear requests without sounding rigid

Why and how do its ingredients work?

Share observations without sounding judgmental:

We are constantly interpreting the world. We tend to find patterns, guess motives and attach meaning to everything around us. While this helps us predict, prepare or prevent; it also makes us preemptive and judgmental. We keep adding notions and biases to the way we perceive a situation, and continue to add flavors and spices to the way we narrate that situation to others or to ourselves. Doing so often impacts the texture of our interpretations and interactions.

On the other hand, if we see ourselves less of a storyteller and more of a reporter (surely not the ones we see on the news channels these days, who in the garb of being reporter are more of a storyteller) then we will see things the way they are, and not the way we would like them to be. This, in turn, will help us state and 'put across' our observations rather than coating them with speculations and quoting them as inferences. This small difference can make a difference.

For instance, there is a difference between saying "It is 5:30 pm, and the meeting-time was at 4:30 pm. Moreover, I remember specifically mentioning that first half an hour of meeting is the most important part of it" and saying "As usual, you are casual about the meeting-time and are late again, and quite predictably, you did not pay heed to my request of coming early for a change". The latter one mixes judgment with observation to sabotage ensuing communication.

Express feelings without tagging the other person:

There is a subtle difference between emotions and feelings. Emotions are physiological specializations that we are born pre-installed with. These physiological specializations are vital for our survival. For example, in fear, the blood flows towards our feet so that we can run; and in anger, the blood flows towards our hands so that we can hit. This 'flight or fight' reaction is a typical example of energy-mobilization (emotion can be seen as 'energy in motion').

On the other hand, feelings are subjective experiences shaped by our thoughts and interpretations. Communicating these experiences with each other is the fabric on which our interpersonal nature is woven. Thus, while it is pivotal to express positive feelings, it is equally vital to express negative feelings like disappointment, disillusionment or disagreeableness. Unexpressed feelings become breeding ground for frustration, friction and factions.

Having said that, communicating one's feelings is a responsible act. It should be done without violating the interpersonal boundaries. This requires carefully choosing words that describe our inner experience, without causing collateral damage by tagging the other person. At the end of the day, our feelings should reach the other person without making them feel labeled, blamed, criticized or devalued. After all, what is the use of expressing feelings if it breeds a vicious circle!

Assert your needs without sounding demanding:

Each one of us has a right to express their need. Whether the other person acknowledges it or not, one's right to convey what matters to them is nonnegotiable. However, not every one of us thinks that way. Due to multiple factors at work – hesitation, shyness, reluctance, politeness, fear of offending someone, or insecurity of coming across as needy – most of us suppress the expression of our needs. Even worse, some start questioning whether they are even legitimate.

On the other hand, some of us operate from a sense of entitlement. They believe as if every other person exists for a utility. Resultantly, they express their needs with an assumption that the unmet ones should've already been addressed. This belief reflects in their communication in the form of a tinge of aggression. When they express a need, they choose their words, tone and gestures in a manner that makes the other one feel as if a demand is being placed on them.

The right thing to do is to express your needs without placing them as demands. More than anything else, it requires careful choice of words. For instance, it is a good idea for a supervisor to say to their team-member something like – "For ten days in a row, your entry in the office has been at least thirty minutes past the scheduled time. When this happens, it violates my need as a supervisor to have my whole team around me at the start of the work day". It works.

Make clear requests without sounding rigid:

There are people who are good at identifying what someone has not done but just can't clarify – in required details – what needs to be done. This always keeps the other person guessing regarding what exactly is expected of them. It is frustrating in a sense that such ambiguity leaves much to be desired. This also takes a toll on the 'trust factor', as the other person finds it tough to take anything on face value and unanswered questions widen the communication gap.

On the other hand, there are people who, in the name of clarity, become so instructive or rude that the other person loses sight of what is being said and gets put off by how it is being said. Their style makes them come across as rigid. With such uncompromising vibe exchanged, the other person either blocks the content sent their way or questions the motive. This has a pretty counterproductive effect on both the ongoing communication as well as the larger equation.

The most apt way to make request for an action or connection is to stay specific and to stay positive in language. It is best to avoid 'should and must' and stay closer to 'would request/like to'. For instance, saying "Would you be willing to stay for extra half an hour in the office today" or "Would you please help me in the kitchen until the cake gets baked" or "Could you kindly create the activity-calendar for this month" will be the best ways to communicate a request.

5

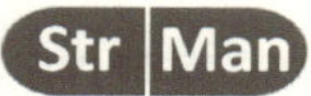

The 'Stress Management' Skill-Pill

What is it about?

Stress, per se, isn't bad; it is its level that makes it good or bad. After all, all works and creations of significance require someone to stretch oneself beyond one's comfort zone, which of course isn't a pretty feeling to start with. However, there is another angle here – perception of one's control over the stressor. If you believe that you have a choice in the matter then stress is, in a way, exhilarating. A good example is how one feels on a rollercoaster – Stressed? Nah!

Two terms by endocrinologist Hans Selye clarify the difference in the best manner – Eustress and Distress (we have talked about it earlier). Eustress is good stress, the one which makes you improve and improvise. Distress is bad stress, the one which deteriorates and damages. The problem is that there is still a lot of subjectivity involved in the differentiation. Eustress for one can be distress for another, and vice versa. This relativity is at the heart of emotional problems.

When it comes to people with intrapersonal and interpersonal challenges, vulnerability in the face of stress is a common aspect. They not only have a lower threshold of stress but also have a lower breaking-point on the continuum of stress tolerance. In all, there is a lack of acceptance towards the inevitability of stress in adult life, and absence of clarity on how to navigate one's thoughts, behaviors, choices and actions. A potent prevention to this is the skill-pill – StrMan.

What are its ingredients?

RED PACK they are:

R – Reappraise scenario rationally

E – Embrace ambiguity maturely

D – Detach misplaced-emotions logically

P – Prioritize tasks sequentially

A – Allocate resources proportionately

C – Converge attention intently

K – Keep working procedurally

Why and how do its ingredients work?

Reappraise scenario rationally:

It won't be wrong to say that stress is prominently 'perceptual'. Yes, to a great deal, it is based on one's perception of the situation oneself is in. So, the same situation could be stressful to one and not so much for someone else. But this is good news, because it typically means that if we can change our perception then a part of stress we feel can be regulated. However, now the question is – what all variables constitute what we are calling 'perception' over here?

Among multiple factors influencing our perception, major would be – level of one's sensitivity, degree of acceptance, extent of imagination, presumed amount of control, estimation of one's resources, and attachment to what is at stake. If you see the list (by no means exhaustive), you would find that, while it isn't possible to change one's sensitivity-level right away, others in the list can be edited or rewritten, if not readily, for sure, relatively quickly (of course with effort).

This process is known as 'reappraisal'. Now, if we talk about how to reappraise, the best part is that if you simply convert all aspects of the list into questions, reappraisal will automatically start. Simply ask – Am I reluctant/ resistant in accepting the situation? Am I basing my inference on evidence/ facts or my notions? Am I assuming lesser control than I actually have? Am I underestimating my internal/ external resources? Am I getting too attached to the outcome?

Embrace ambiguity maturely:

Stress typically rides the vehicle of uncertainty. When the information is limited and clarity is compromised then we feel a surge of discomfort inside. However, adult life is all about leaving the shore of certainty and embarking on the journey of exploration. Trained in the controlled (almost regimented) ecosystem of school and family right through one's childhood, most people find the contrast unbearable. This internal craving for constants is at the heart of stress.

In absence of the clearly laid out series of data, decision-making feels excruciating. You feel a burden of loneliness and accountability. That's where the virtue of 'maturity' features in the equation. Maturity can be understood best through the words of Fitzgerald – *"The test of a first-rate intelligence is the ability to hold two opposing ideas in the mind at the same time, and still retain the ability to function"*; and this can only happen when you embrace ambiguity.

Embracing ambiguity brings with it a gift of many new skills. It liberates you from the shackles of control, and helps you imbibe the all-important wisdom of focusing on the process and relinquishing the desire to control the results. This simple shift in paradigm can improve your sanity and serenity, best described in the words – *"God, grant me the serenity to accept what I cannot change, the courage to change what I can, and the wisdom to know the difference"*.

Detach misplaced-emotions logically:

A major problem with stress is that it invokes inside us a gamut of emotions. While some of them are natural and utile, most are neither contextually relevant nor required in a situational sense. These misplaced emotions often act as noise in the signal. They consume a part of our cognitive bandwidth that could have been allocated more fruitfully for reappraising scenario or searching for solutions. Having said that, it all starts with spotting the misplaced emotions.

For instance, if you are under the stress of solving a health problem, it is natural to feel some sadness and worry. However, imagine that you start feeling guilt for ignoring your health earlier and then begin feeling a lot of anger towards the factors that kept you occupied and did not let you focus on what mattered to you. Now, if you see, while doing some of it would be inevitable, getting drowned in this downward spiral of 'guilt and anger' isn't going to help your cause at all.

It is only going to act as a deterrent to 'what needs to be done now' (worse, if you don't focus on what matters now then it will later become seed for another loop of guilt and anger). So you see, not all that one feels is logical and fruitful. What's important is the deliberate practice of segregating which emotions are useful and which are misplaced. Again, the moment you begin to intentionally look at your emotions with an analytical eye, the mist starts to get dispelled.

Prioritize tasks sequentially:

Human mind has an inherent preference and liking for orderliness and structure. After all, brain is essentially a predictive organ. It evolved to help us anticipate, prepare and prospect. It simply loves the world of Standard Operating Procedure (SOP) and Codes of Conduct

(COC), as they help our sensory sentinels to drop their constant guard and switch from the metabolically expensive 'flight or fight' mode to the mode of 'resting and digesting; feeding and breeding'.

When we are under stress, suddenly there is a chaos outside as well as inside. Whatever was decided has to be now reevaluated. As a result, mind faces two challenges simultaneously. On one hand, it has to deal with the sense of disillusionment born out of the loss of predictability. On the other hand, it has to now deal with a blend of nervousness, discomfort and irritability that come in the wake of a realization – 'now you got to decipher it all, all over again'.

In such a scenario, it is a fairly good idea to follow the dictum of 'putting first things first', that is, to differentiate between urgent and important, and then see what's urgent as well as important. Once such priorities have been identified, now is a good time to convert them into tasks that are, as George Doran famously called them, SMART (Specific, Measurable, Attainable, Relevant and Time-bound). Now sequence such tasks, and you have your starting point.

Allocate resources proportionately:

When we talk about the term 'management', it is essentially about allocation and utilization of resources. For instance, in business management, it is about working with six major resources – men (as a gender-neutral word), machine, money, material, methods and mother-nature (natural resources). Even in intrapersonal terms, the management of stress will again boil down to allocation of resources, however, in this case, cognitive and emotional resources.

Which cognitive and emotional resources are we talking about? Well, they are time, energy, attention, memory (together, you can see them as our internal TEAM that we work with). These are the channels through which our mental energy flows (and in a way, stress is about mental energy getting stuck). Though far-fetched, this concept can also be seen through the lens of an old psychoanalytical term 'Cathexis' – concentration of mental energy on a particular entity.

For instance, if we are stressed, we have to be mindful of our temporal orientation, i.e. where is our time getting invested? Being meticulously aware of the passage of time and on what are we spending our hours is the first step. Then the same real-time auditing has to be done for our energy (physical as well as mental), attention and memory. Once we have done it, the key is to allocate our internal team to our most important priorities (refer to the last section).

Converge attention intently:

Of all the resources we discussed in the last section, viz. time, energy, attention and memory, the most critical one is our 'attention'. In a way, our attention almost drags all other resources towards the direction it chooses to take. It is almost akin to a torch. When you point a torch towards something, it gets well-lit, and precisely that's where discretion needs to be exercised. So the point is – where do we deploy our attention so that the stress is managed aptly?

To answer this question, let's first understand what happens to attention when we get stressed. Well, first our attention converges on to the stressor. Everything else becomes less visible and all we care about is what is causing us stress. However, contrary dynamics are also at work. As we think about how to address the stressor, our attention tends to get divergent, and we begin to randomly think about multiple aspects. This dispersion of attention makes us feel helpless.

So the key is to stay convergent but on the right aspect. This will first require taking attention away from the stressor. This disengagement of attention from the stressor will free other resources of our internal team. Now, the next step is to de-clutter. We need to zoom-in on that 'one aspect' we have prioritized and ensure that all other parts are blurred. This convergence then allows us to work on the stressor without creating more stress in the process of doing so.

Keep working procedurally:

If you look at people who are effectively pursuing any high-stress job, you would find one thing common– they are less of creatures of choices and more of creatures of habits. Most act almost on auto-pilot mode. One thing stacked after another, their schedule (and at times even behavior) looks almost algorithmic. There are pre-fed if-then conditions, with possible decision-points predicted in advance and even the courses of action fed into a drop-down menu of sorts.

Why is it so? Is it an effort to dehumanize? Is it an effort to mechanize? No. Rather it is actually an effort to standardize, so that the effect (the result) is separated from affect (the emotions). It becomes even more important amid stress because, often, the stakes are high and resources are low. At that time, it is risky to tap into one's motivation and craft, as both operate in some abstraction and thus are vulnerable to variation. It is better to bank on the good old 'process'.

So, just compartmentalize, and execute the apt steps aptly. Wait. But for that, you got to have clarity on what the steps are. This typically means that it is always good to have a plan in place – a plan to follow when things don't go as per the plan. It will require some scenario planning (imagining possible situations in considerable details) in advance, and practicable steps that can be reduced to the last degree of controllable actions. Then, it is all about following the same.

6

Sen | Man

The 'Sensitivity Management' Skill-Pill

What is it about?

Sensitivity can be seen as the ability to stay in tune with one's environment and react real-time to the stimuli with intensity. In other words, sensitive people observe more acutely, absorb more vividly, store more strongly, process more connectedly and retrieve more readily. They are very 'emotionally responsive' to any inputs, specifically the ones that involve 'change'. As a result, they are quick to cry, laugh, feel hurt, get offended, empathize, reach out, and adapt.

This heightened 'sensory processing' of stimulation and information is a hallmark of what are called HSPs (Highly Sensitive Persons). The term was coined by Elaine and Arthur Aron, and roughly 15 to 20 percent of the population is believed to have high sensitivity. These people get overwhelmed easily, avoid stressful situations, pick up on nuances, are sensitive to pain and often aim to please others. Among other factors, genetic predisposition has a part to play here.

When it comes to people with intrapersonal and interpersonal challenges, high sensitivity is a common point. In fact, it is believed that most of the psychologists' clients come from the pool of HSPs. Understandably so, because while their sensitivity is a rare gift, hardware of the world doesn't really support their software. So, for them, it is a continuous struggle to not only 'adjust and adapt' but to 'survive and thrive'. A potent support to this is the skill-pill – **SenMan.**

What are its ingredients?

SOMBERNESS they are:

S – Separation of tasks

O – Over-commitment caution

M – Multitasking avoidance

B – Boundary formation

E – Exposure limiting

R – Routine sanctity

N – Nonjudgmental/Nonalignment policy

E – Emotion-outlet mechanism

S – Selectiveness in company

S – Stepwise approach to actions

Why and how do its ingredients work?

Separation of tasks:

People who are high on sensitivity often have a tendency to own other people's responsibility. In fact, in general, they feel that they are responsible for almost everything and everyone. What is worse is that even after they take others' responsibility, they still feel responsible for others' feelings. Now it is obvious that you can never have absolute control over how others feel; so eventually they feel overwhelmed, stressed, disillusioned, devalued or simply tired of all of it.

Legendary psychologist Alfred Adler (who unfortunately got overshadowed by two of his more known contemporaries Sigmund Freud and Carl Jung) talked about a very important concept in his domain of 'Individual Psychology' – Separation of tasks. According to him, it is important to ask "Whose task is this?" or "Who eventually benefits from this task?" as the answers to these questions help you abstain from intervening in others' tasks and in focusing intently on yours.

On surface, this could come across as selfishness or isolation but, in fact, it is exactly opposite. It fosters a sense of accountability born out of autonomy and mutual respect. It becomes even more important in the close relationships because that's precisely from where sensitive people invite most of their load. They keep assuming responsibility even of the tasks that aren't theirs.

Mindfully separating tasks frees them of needless burden and helps them pick their priorities.

Over-commitment caution:

Probably the most common trait of sensitive people is the inability to say 'No'. They find it very difficult to deny any request for help or any delegation of responsibility directed towards them. There are two reasons for this. First, they think that their 'No' might offend the other person in some way (it is almost as if they project their own sensitivity in the other person). Second, they feel genuine compassion and a sense of moral responsibility in most interpersonal situations.

Resultantly, they often end up committing too much, too early, on too many fronts. Yes, they say yes, and then push themselves beyond their resources, often at the risk of causing burnout. It becomes a vicious circle of 'failing to assess feasibility', 'flailing to somehow come close to the commitment', 'falling short of expectations (others' and their own)', and 'feeling bad about what they could not do but believe they should have done'. This gradually becomes a pattern.

This is quite avoidable if you keep two tools ready in your behavioral toolkit – assertiveness and analysis. It is crucial to stay forthright and direct without being aggressive and abrasive. Also, it is critical to rationally (and holistically) assess feasibility of a task before committing. It involves scenario planning in the light of resources and situations. It is vital, as over-commitment eventually creates more problems than it solves, and that too for all stakeholders in a situation.

Multitasking avoidance:

Multitasking is now a norm. People are not only savoring it or taking pride in it, but also getting addicted to it. Well, from the perspective of neuroscience, multitasking is a myth (in terms of cognitive tasks) because brain actually does 'switch-tasking', and every time it does it, it loses effectiveness at the cost of efficiency, and more importantly, to a sensitive person, it brings what is called 'frontal fatigue' (tiredness of our brain's centers for higher order functions).

As a result, they get frazzled. Yes, they are so exhausted and strained that now even the easiest of tasks seems burdensome – priorities get all muddled up, focus becomes a thing of the past, decisions look like huge dilemmas, senses start capturing all sorts of information from the environment, and doing even the most obvious thing requires disproportionate amount of will power. And all this happens because they took up the ambitious task of multitasking.

Thus, an important priority of a sensitive person is to avoid multitasking at all costs; and even when it is unavoidable, it is crucial that they rationalize expectations, ritualize the courses of action, slow down the pace of the game, assess the progress regularly, and keep a track of their intrapersonal state. They should also group similar tasks, so that they make multitasking as light as possible metabolically. Moreover, they must take regular breaks for their behavioral balance.

Boundary formation:

The fact is that all healthy relationships have clear boundaries. Though it would sound ironical, boundaries render freedom, as people involved in the relationship or association find it easy to form their territories of actions and choices. There is less ambiguity and more breathing space. People know what to expect, and such predictability facilitates trust. Moreover, what people generally don't understand is that boundaries are not based on selfishness but on 'respect'.

Only when you truly respect other person's individuality, you can value your own. Seen through that lens, boundaries are statements of mutual respect. They don't restrict, they protect. Here, it is important to establish that "all healthy relationships have boundaries without borders". So, boundaries are not rigid, they are just clear. There is no effort to guard one's fences or see the other side as threat. There is interdependence without sacrificing respective independence(s).

For sensitive people, it becomes even more important because they often lack assertiveness to continuously remind people of what affects them and how much. They also tend to suffer discomfort in silence. So it doesn't hurt if you clarify that – "I keep Sundays strictly for family" or "I don't answer calls before 10 am and after 8 pm". But then, it's equally important to also ask – "What are your preferred timings for taking an official call". See, it works both ways!

Exposure limiting:

The most characteristic quality of sensitive people is that they tend to pay attention to minutest aspects in their environment and then process the observed sensory inputs very vividly. While it can be seen as a superpower that they possess, it also makes the world an overwhelming place for them, because they are all the time inundated by a huge amount of data coming their way, and are absorbed continuously in voluntarily as well as involuntarily processing that data.

This often leaves them exhausted as well as exasperated. However, the problem is that they cannot 'not do' it. They are simply wired that way. So now it boils down to how to channelize this extraordinary gift that has been bestowed upon them? The most logical way is to narrow down area of their observation so that curtailing of width can translate into detailing in depth. It is on the lines of the saying "specialization is to know more and more about less and less".

Having said that, it is not easy for a sensitive person to do so, as they feel almost a pathological pull towards what's going on around them. What doctor orders is real increase in will-power on the person's part! By choosing what they have access to (social media or news channels) and who has access to them (community and contacts), they can turn their trait into strength. What helps additionally is to know what their triggers are, and to safeguard oneself against them.

Routine sanctity:

Just the way a moving train travels on a static track, a person's schedule, in many ways, decides the smoothness of movement of their life. This temporal aspect of life is often ignored by us, at our own peril. See it this way! Only humans have got the constructive curse of daily deciding what to do with the duration between the sunrise and sunset. All other animals have their job cut out. They focus on their regular activities, with clear two goals – survival and procreation.

Blame it on the newest (and the most advanced) part of human brain - Neocortex – we have a variety of higher-order intellect-based jobs like preparation, patience and creativity to choose from. It goes without saying that, while picking our favorites from the buffet of activities, like any other animal, we are still supposed to also take care of our baseline survival functions. This is what makes human life stressful in a unique way, and creates an everyday decision-fatigue.

Handling this stress is tougher for highly sensitive people as they already have high vulnerability towards change. This is what makes it even more important for them to have a clear schedule for a specific day. Even if it is derived from monthly or weekly timelines, or is subject to change according to circumstances, keeping a sense of 'flow' for a day makes it easier for a person to allocate external and internal resources, and an outcome of it is improved 'emotional stability'.

<u>N</u>onjudgmental/Nonalignment policy:

Sensitive people have almost a compulsive need to stay attuned to their environment, and since the most variable component in any environment is 'people', they constantly observe their behavior, absorb their energies, perceive their stands, estimate their actions, and calibrate the equations between people. This not only creates sensory overload for sensitive people but also leads to a continuous pursuit of adjusting how people are positioned in their head.

While this is a natural thing to be done by all humans (it is not for nothing that the default-act for human brain in any downtime – when it isn't doing anything deliberate – is taking a stock of how we are doing in all the relationships that matter to us), for sensitive people, it takes more cognitive and emotional bandwidth than it usually should. This gets even more consuming if notions of 'right and wrong' or 'good and bad' are attached, as then it needs more processing.

Thus, to regulate stress or anxiety, the preferred stance for sensitive people towards the world at large should be to remain as nonjudgmental as possible. Even when they are supposed to take sides, as long as possible (and without getting labeled as indecisive or indifferent), they should try to maintain nonalignment, because even the most casual debates or harmless tussles tend to disturb the emotional homeostasis of sensitive people, causing a lot of over-thinking.

Emotion-outlet mechanism:

As we discussed earlier, emotion can be seen as 'energy in motion'. This energy, if unreleased or unconverted, creates a sort of internal pressure in our intra-psychic system. You can feel this pressure in the form of an underlying anxiety or a disproportionate reaction to something quite harmless. It is a way of our system to let us know that we are sitting on something unresolved or unexpressed. This phenomenon is only more pronounced in people with higher sensitivity.

As they absorb more and accommodate or avoid more, they tend to store and suffer more. It is a typical characteristic of sensitive people. Often, they are sitting on a volcano, pretending that all is under control. However, it only takes a bad day or a phase when things start piling up one after another, and you will find that illusion of control gets shattered in a matter of moments, as if that one opening was all that was needed to get all the pent-up energy released.

To counter this, sensitive people need to have a mechanism to give outlet to their emotions and feelings. The best two are sports and arts. Sports were, in a way, invented by society as a substitute for war, so that the violent streak inside humans can find regular release. Arts like writing and painting can give words to the feelings, and ones like dance can combine the benefits of arts and sports. However, nothing beats the good old 'talking to a confidant'. Try it!

Selectiveness in company:

It is now almost an established conclusion that social connections are as important to us as oxygen (that's why solitary confinement behind a wall is seen as the harshest punishment). Yes, our interpersonal bonds have immense power to facilitate our delighting, healing, resurgence, balancing, encouragement and empowerment. In fact, researches even show that people who live in groups tend to have greater immunity, less stress, and better overall health.

But this was only one part of the story. Most of our suffering also comes from relationships – the heartbreak, backstabbing, betrayal, shortchanging, and what not! Isn't that ironical? Well, that's how it is; can't help it. So you see, the difference lies in the kind of people and the quality of relationships. In short, good relationships have good effect on us, and bad relationships have bad effect on us. That's why, in every culture, emphasis is placed on choosing right company.

Naturally, for sensitive people, it becomes even more important to be selective with people, as they absorb energies, vibes and aura of people through subtle emotional transactions in the form of micro-expressions, prosodic features and smallest of changes in postures and gestures. In this emotional contagion, sensitive people are often impacted deeply; and more so if they are less assertive when they should be. So remember! Not everyone has a seat on the bus.

Stepwise approach to actions:

What overwhelms us can always be divided and brought to a level where it becomes less awful and more manageable. That's the power of division in reference to a vision. This concept is at the heart of management across all the domains – yearly objectives are broken into quarterly goals, which then are further broken into month-end targets and then weekly task-sheets. It works on two fronts – first, in terms of measurement, and second, in terms of motivation.

They say "what cannot be measured cannot be managed". True! One needs to have clarity on the criteria of evaluation and timeline of inspection. It is required to make work countable and people accountable. Moreover, when we are able to divide destinations into milestones, it is easier to maintain motivation, as to our brain, the frequency of success matters more than the size of success. So when we rejoice milestone-accomplishment, morale is sustained throughout.

Aforementioned logics call for a stepwise approach to actions, where progressively sequential distribution of task gives clarity on what needs to be done in the current coordinates of time and space. While it works for all sorts of people, it is most useful for sensitive people, as they get anxious with the lengths and breadths of tasks. Their ever-active imagination is sensitized further and leads to nervousness. The solution lies in a stepwise approach to actions.

7

The 'Conflict Resolution' Skill-Pill

What is it about?

We live in a social apparatus that is not easy to navigate through. It requires a constant effort on our part to negotiate between 'what we want to do' and 'what we need to do'. Whether we talk in intra-psychic or inter-psychic terms, this clash is at the heart of being human. Specifically in the 'partly hierarchical partly democratic' webbing of our social and professional domains, people's priorities are bound to be at odds with each other, creating face-offs all the time.

In other words, conflicts are inevitable; either they are happening or are waiting to happen. It's just that the magnitude varies. What also varies is people's attitude towards conflict. Some like to avoid conflict at all costs and some relish a good fight. Either extreme is unhealthy, and the most functional strategy is to move the mental knob smoothly between the two ends to suit the situation as well as the purpose. After all, this is the litmus test of being social beings!

So, our ability to resolve conflicts is what makes us socially well-adjusted and interpersonally well-suited. Constructive push-pull and subsequent cordiality are hallmarks of maturity. On the other hand, people with intrapersonal and interpersonal issues are often unable to appreciate both the inevitability and the utility of conflict. It probably happens because they are not sure if they can regulate it and then resolve it. A potent prevention to this is the skill-pill – **ConRes.**

What are its ingredients?

SALIENCE they are:

S – Stay focused on the goals

A – Avoid getting sucked into the argument

L – Let the other person speak

I – Input the feedback on the behavior, not on the person

E – Explain your points in a calm yet confident way

N – Negotiate patiently for a win–win

C – Control the unwanted threads in the discussion

E – End on a forward-looking note

Why and how do its ingredients work?

Stay focused on the goals:

Conflict resolution essentially involves communication (of course, it doesn't mean only talking and talking but also a sense of what, when, where, and how much).

What most people don't realize is that what separates communication from conversation is goal-orientation. In fact, what often derails any effort of resolving conflict is the absence of goal, less clarity on goal, lack of agreement on goal, attempt to chase too many goals simultaneously, or simply wrong goals.

For instance, in an interaction, if your goal is to move forward, you cannot backtrack and dig old graves; if your goal is to make someone feel good then you cannot start with a mention of the mistakes made by the other person; if your goal is to mend something broken then you cannot start by revising what had happened; if your goal is to extend a heartfelt apology then you cannot digress and talk about how the other person's behavior triggered that somehow.

In other words, it is important to ensure that what you say stays relevant. However, it is not only about the verbal part but also about the nonverbal part. If your tone, pitch or volume, or for that matter, your gestures, postures and expressions betray even in subtlest of ways, the alignment suffers, and so does the effort to resolve conflict. Beware! All this cannot be done with piecemeal approach, what's required is conceptual awareness, and rest all follows.

Avoid getting sucked into the argument:

Invitation to be a part of an argument is arguably one of the toughest things to decline. The offer is almost irresistible, because when someone is looking right at you with intensity and momentum, a part of you wants to get carried away and join the freaky show of logic-flexing which is backed by the primal desire for one-upmanship. After all, all of us are secretly waiting to return to our animal selves and feel the freedom of living by anything but the book.

However, this is exactly what must be avoided at all costs. The reason is simple – once the slugfest starts, coming back to senses is an activity that becomes metabolically very expensive for the brain. It has to allocate its meager resources to fight a battle that is naturally appealing to the lower layers of the brain. The parts of the brain responsible for higher order functions have a hard time trying to think straight while fighting the urge to relish the release.

Thus it is always better to not get tempted in the first place. After all, we all know some places are best avoided, Isn't it? There is no one prescribed way to do it. You got to find your own way that matches the situation and works well with the person you are pitted against. Do whatever it takes (you will find a lot of ways discussed elsewhere in the book) but don't join the futile act of arm-wrestling, even if you feel you come across as someone who was not up for it.

Let the other person speak:

Most conflicts start because one person feels that the other one doesn't care. This feeling of a lack of care can come from various routes like "he doesn't give me attention or time" or "she doesn't try to see things from my point of view" or "he is trying to take advantage of my situation" or "she is trying to take me for granted" or "he is insensitive towards me", and more such thought-threads leading to the same conclusion that "the other person doesn't care".

In addition to this underlying theme, another factor is at work, specifically when the conflict is playing out in the form of an angry monologue or a heated debate. This factor can be termed as 'energy mobilization'. During the verbal confrontation, energy starts getting mobilized inside. It keeps increasing in a winding manner, especially due to the eye-contact (that too an intense one, which is a characteristic feature of conflict) and an animated nonverbal behavior.

Now, if we see closely, both the abovementioned points can be addressed skillfully through one simple act – letting the other person speak. It has twin benefits. While an uninterrupted flow of thoughts and words can help the other person feel a sense of energy-release (provided you do not make strange faces while it is happening), letting the other person speak also helps you earn brownie points on criteria of empathy, respect and patience. In the end, they all add up.

Input the feedback on the behavior, not on the person:

In general, people find it quite hard to see themselves separate from their actions, behaviors and attitudes. They assume that all of them are bundled together to form their identity. While it is quite logical to see it that way, it creates a peculiar difficulty for someone who is giving any input to them – whatever is said to them about their actions, behaviors or attitudes is seen as a comment on the 'kind of person' they are. Understandably, as a result, they get defensive.

There lies one of the roots of conflict. We all are forever on guard corresponding to anything that targets us. It is so much a part of our subconscious firewall that we do it without realizing it (in fact, often rationalizing it later by coming up with some random reason). So when you give input to others (during the conflict or even when someone is predicting a possible conflict), the biggest challenge is that they are already ready with all the defenses in place.

While you can't do anything to have this tendency obliterated absolutely, you can minimize it by changing the way in which you communicate the input. A good way is to avoid labeling the person, and prefer remarking on the behavior. For example, rather than saying "you are being rude", it is better to say "I find this tone rude", and even better to say "a less emotionally charged tone will help me respond more aptly". The key is to separate the act from the actor.

Explain your points in a calm yet confident way:

During any interpersonal interaction with connotations of conflict, often people experience an emotional contagion. People subliminally catch each other's behavioral cues and start matching each other's attitudinal approach. For instance, when one person starts raising their voice, the other one, even after some effort to not do so, eventually surrenders to the contagious pull and begins to speak in a similar volume. The ensuing slugfest then takes its own course.

An understanding of this phenomenon entrusts us with two tasks – to not unknowingly become a victim of this infectiousness, and also to not be the culprit who starts this slugfest. On the contrary, the contagion can be used constructively. After all, if someone can follow our negative lead then it holds true for the positive one as well. For instance, if you talk in a calm way, with appropriate gestures and posture, the other person will also take a leaf out of your book.

Having said that, there is a caveat here! Calmness can also be misread by some as timidity. The key is to separate the two by blending sufficient characteristics of 'confidence' in our behavior. This has to be done primarily through your nonverbal behavior. A soft yet consistent eye contact, surefooted posture, clear expressions and apt gestures; all together give an impression of deep conviction in what's said. Needless to say, the best way to show it is to have it.

<u>Negotiate patiently for a win-win:</u>

It is useless to come up with a cosmetic solution to a real conflict. What's the use of 'consider it closed' impression when one of the parties is walking away with a sense of grudge? In fact, it is quite dangerous because it will now lead to pent-up emotions that will create not only malice but also manipulation. This is counterproductive as it defeats the whole purpose that, in a sense, conflict psychologically serves – to bring to surface something that was floating beneath.

That's why it is important to see conflict as opportunity to repair whatever was broken – trust, confidence, communication or communion. This repairing cannot be done unless you are ready to forego any solution which is not 'win-win'. Often this commitment for symbiosis and synergy is itself a great conflict resolver, as when the other person observes this then there is a natural desire to reciprocate. After all, humans do have an intuitive inclination for interdependence.

While it is a worthy goal, attaining this win–win is not easy. People generally start with some degree of cynicism and a sense of self-preservation riding high. It requires patient remolding of thoughts and behavior to change the goal. At the core, it is a consistent process of negotiation, i.e. two persons carrying out a real-time 'push- pull'. 'You' have to start it with resolve, and then carry it on with astuteness backed by analysis, lateral thinking, adaptability and articulation.

Control the unwanted threads in the discussion:

In the name of civilization, we have created an ecosystem that forces us to comply with norms of good-bad and right-wrong. Most of us abide by them most of the time. For instance, even when we are upset with something, we tend to push our emotional ripples and thought threads into our subconscious. However, they don't go anywhere. They are lurking around, waiting for the first opportunity to ride any outgoing emotions that match them in texture or context.

A conflict gives them just the right kind of opportunity – emotions are riding high, a sense of being shortchanged is felt, and a feeling of vindication is chased. While it is good news for the hidden unprocessed content inside us, it is bad news for our current goal of resolving conflict, prominently because they interfere with feelings and thoughts and color perception in a way that is shaped more by what is inside people and less by what is happening between them.

This 'ghost from the past' is visible through unwanted threads in the discussion. For example, while arguing about which venue to choose for hosting a party, suddenly a spouse begins to talk about how she hasn't ever got enough respect for her opinions and wishes. While spotting such a thread is vital, it is equally vital to demonstrate the required maturity in words and behavior to also help the other person in not only identifying but also filtering it (without taking offense).

We mostly remember our experiences more in terms of the beginnings and the ends than what happened typically in between. You can call it the 'primacy and recency' effect. It gives us a good tip to structure an experience by starting strong and finishing firm. It is equally applicable to the process of conflict resolution, as the way it culminates essentially gives us the starting point of how the relationship or association will fare from here on.

Thus it is crucial to curate one culmination for another commencement. For example, what is the use of keeping maturity throughout the conversation and then ending it with a sour word of cynicism; or for that matter, keeping aside the ego throughout the conflict and then declaring that all got resolved because of your act of sacrifice? It ruins all the hard work. So remember that "it is not over till it is over", and keep the good work going even at the time of going!

It is easier said than done, because by the time any conversation or discussion has reached the end, those who are involved in it have already consumed their mental and physical energy. Towards the fag end, the guards are down and a sense of normalness has resumed. It is exactly the point at which the suppressed feelings and regulated content find their way out. So, see someone off with a feeling of cordiality and a message for synergy and mutuality.

8

The 'Impulse Control' Skill-Pill

What is it about?

We all get pulled into the prospect of unleashing ourselves time to time. It is nothing new; we all, as social animals, have experienced that itch to set ourselves free and have it our way. The animal behind our social veil is after all always ready to break the shackles of 'right and wrong' or 'good and bad'. It waves strongest for the desire of 'here and now' – proverbial 'immediate gratification'. Sadly (but not ironically), it is far stronger for personal gain than for greater good.

This inability to delay gratification is behind the hot-blooded actions of inappropriateness, dishonesty, violation and cruelty. Stephen Covey says – "Between the stimulus and response lies the freedom to choose" but this intervention of free will is blocked by the overwhelming force of our animal brain that holds its sway on us in a way that our rationality never can. In such a moment, we become the most irrational self-serving version of us, slave to the push of passion.

When it comes to people with intrapersonal and interpersonal challenges, inability to control impulse is a characteristic feature. They surrender to their impulse more readily than others. It is as if a part of them is priming them to sabotage their control at the drop of a hat, and most of them fall prey to that so naturally that they begin to lose confidence in their ability to weather the storm that emerges inside. A potent prevention to this is the skill-pill – **ImpCon.**

What are its ingredients?

POWER they are:

P – Pause mentally as well as physically

O – Occlude the sensory inputs

W – Withdraw into your headspace

E – Explicitly ask for time to respond

R – Redirect your nervous energy

Why and how do its ingredients work?

Pause mentally as well as physically:

What people don't realize is that pausing is not an act, it is a skill. This will come across as quite counterintuitive because we have been conditioned to believe that we pause on our own and that there is no voluntary hand behind the act. While it is correct in one sense (we have come pre-wired by evolution to 'freeze' in certain situations), in another sense, a 'mindful pause' is not an act that happens on its own, we need to continue to do it to be able to do it effortlessly.

A part of it comes from pausing physically (after all, emotions are not some abstract conceptual constructs; they are physiological specializations that one can feel within one's body). Haven't you seen people gazing laterally in response to a query, frozen in an expression, and then gradually making their way back into the conversation with a far more measured deliberate manner of speaking? Well, that's the kind of pausing that I am talking about – voluntary.

And then there is a mental angle to it. You got to simply 'stay put', halting the cognitive process inside your head, and not supplying mental energy to any thought thread (least of all the one that is trying to hijack your mind in the current moment). It is not something that can be done right away. It requires a history of having done it before – whether through focused-attention meditation or repeatedly trying to do so in low-stake situations until you can regulate it at will.

Occlude the sensory inputs:

So how did the impulse emerge inside you? Typically due to two factors at work – internal and external. In the previous point, we talked about keeping a check on what is going inside, now is the turn to keep a check on what in your environment triggered the impulse and is now fueling it. It could be someone's words or tone or expression or gestures or posture; or for that matter what is transpiring right in front of you and is causing you some sort of emotional stimulation.

Whatever it is, it is crucial to block those inputs to stop the supply-chain of impulse–aggravating material. Take your eyes off it or block the sound by walking away or refuse to engage in skin contact, whatever can be done within the norms of civilized behavior in the situation should be executed right away. A failure to do so leads to a scenario of potential escalation, and once you reach the 'point of no return', there is no coming back and soon all hell is bound to break loose.

A good example is that of 'road rage'. Although social, we humans are still animals, and like most animals, we are territorial and don't like intrusion in our space or violation of boundaries that causes hurt or harm. When a fellow driver on the road rubs us the wrong way, even the most sophisticated people lose control and get into a fistfight. In such situation, the first thing to be done is to avoid an 'eye to eye' contact, as it charges both up like no other thing can.

<u>Withdraw into your headspace:</u>

While introspection is the last thing your impulse will let you do when it is reigning supreme, even a semblance of it can bring great benefit. What is introspection? At heart, it is an attempt to withdraw into your own headspace and evaluate your attitudes, behaviors or actions in reference to your values, benchmarks or goals. Needless to say, it works wonders in reorienting one's thoughts and emotions. No surprise it is highly regarded in sphere of self-management!

It is understandable that you can't ask existential questions when emotions are holding their sway, yet just one fundamental question that can make you sit up and take notice of what is going on can go a long way in taking some pinch away from the prick. The question can be - "What is making me mad about this whole scenario?"; "Why am I getting worked up about such a silly thing?"; "Am I so weak that I can't let just a few minutes pass without invoking reaction?"

One such question, if it hits the sweet-spot in our consciousness, has a potential to change the pivot. Suddenly you have a flash of insight conveying stuff like – "I have put the hard yards, and can't do something foolish to throw it all away in a rush of blood"; "Hang on! It is just a set of words that the other person is speaking. Let me not act on some verbal abstraction"; "There is a lot riding on my ability to stomach the inconvenience of staying silent. Let me respect it".

Explicitly ask for time to respond:

While writing this, what is flashing in front of my eyes is the 'T' sign that sportsmen make with their hands to call a 'Time out'! It serves such an important purpose. Captains use it to slow the pace of the game, or to break the momentum of the opponent, or to reorient the focus of the players, or to simply press some imaginary 'F5' button on the mental keyboard, or to go back to the drawing board and re-strategize, or to take stock of what is working and what is not.

Again, justifiably it is not always possible to ask for a break. It can come across as anything between naïve to rude. However, whenever possible and contextually not inapt, one can say something like "Can we take a short break and resume the discussion afterwards?", or "Can we hold on for a minute, I think the heat of the discussion is getting to me", or even something as peculiar as "I guess I am about to say something that I might regret later, so let me let it pass".

This can change the texture of circumstance by giving everyone a 'cooling off' opportunity. Even those who find it strange at the time tend to realize the value of it later. In fact, sometimes one of the parties to the discussion could well be thinking of doing so but probably was too shy to attempt it. It also establishes you as a 'mature mind' who also knows when to pull away. In all, if timed properly, communicated aptly and utilized fruitfully, this is quite a helpful strategy.

Redirect your nervous energy:

An impulse can be seen as a sudden thrust of energy, primed to take one towards a certain course of action. This energy-burst tends to converge your attention-resource, and the body's whole orientation is shifted. People stare at each other; have their torsos facing each other; point fingers at each other; make a physical move in each other's direction; and listen to every word selectively for even the remotest of match with their assumed 'Me vs. They' theme.

This energy is a raw force which cannot be stomached at that point in time. In fact, an attempt to sit on it can, in some cases, bring a health scare. The only way out is to bring it out somehow. Have you seen that stress-ball with a smiley on it? What purpose does it serve? Well, it helps you release the muscular tension (by pressing it, repeatedly making it bounce, or changing the hand that holds it) that your body develops as a result of the activation of 'flight or fight' mode.

Similar actions can be chosen to redirect the nervous energy that is piling up inside. It could be an act as insignificant as pursing lips, stroking chin, rubbing forehead, playing with a keychain, interlocking fingers, pressing the floor with foot, shaking a leg rhythmically; or even a larger movement like standing up and stretching a little or walking intently. Irrespective of the act, the underlying logic is to redirect the energy in installments so that impulse doesn't have its way.

9

The '**Apt Rep**resentation' Skill-Pill

What is it about?

As social animals, our survival has always hinged on our potential to connect and communicate with others. That's why, even today, when we have come a long way in our civilization journey, we still care about how people are, what their equations with each other are, how we would like to be perceived by them, and how they end up perceiving us. Interestingly, for this, we do not depend only on words. We largely (though unconsciously) focus on the nonverbal cues.

We have already discussed that emotions are a set of physiological specializations that we have come pre-wired with. Evolution has given us this toolkit so that, like any other species, we can fulfill the evolutionary goals of survival and procreation. That's why emotions find a bodily way of getting unleashed and we all possess an intuitive eye to interpret someone's emotional state through their physical movements, which taken together, form one's representation.

In any interpersonal space, the way people represent themselves makes a great impact on the actions they take and the reactions they invoke or receive. Seen closely, the people who have emotional or interpersonal issues are generally found challenged on this front, and thus fare poorly in all the situations requiring soft skills. They are just not able to represent themselves in an appropriate manner. A potent prevention to this is the skill-pill – AptRep.

What are its ingredients?

GAME PLANS they are:

G – Gestures flowing

A – Articulation well-placed

M – Mannerism relaxed

E – Expressions stable

P – Posture upright

L – Looking at listener(s)

A – Approach frontal

N – Nodding natural

S – Spatiality proper

Why and how do its ingredients work?

Gestures flowing:

Visualize any person you consider as confident and now try to picture how that person's hands move while speaking or talking. In all probability, you are picturing a person whose hands are moving in sync with the content they are speaking; movements preceding the words by just a moment or two. Vertically, the movements are typically above the waistline, and horizontally, they are typically within or around the imaginary lines drawn around the shoulder-level.

Now visualize any person you consider as diffident and try to picture how that person's hands move while speaking or talking. In all probability, you are picturing a person whose hands are either not moving at all or are manipulating some part of the body or an external object. So there is a lot of holding, scratching, picking, rubbing or grooming. Moreover, even if hands are moving, if the person is not emotionally invested in the content, the sync just isn't there.

Yes, 'gestures flowing effortlessly, in resonance with one's verbal content' is vital characteristic feature of a person who is in control of themselves or situation. These gestures are generally pertaining to shoulders, arms, wrists, hands and fingers; and beyond a point, they can't be regulated at will. That's why, for apt representation, you have to let them be free and do their own thing, and regulate them only when you feel that your thoughts are changing for worse.

Articulation well-placed:

There is always a difference between 'what is said' and 'how it is said', and often, how something is said holds the essence of what was supposed to be conveyed. Yes, human beings are giftedly capable of manipulating their voice to communicate various meanings. Prosody is the term used to describe the variations in the voice that go along with speech and help to convey its meaning. The most important prosodic features are pitch, volume, tempo and thrust.

Pitch can be understood as the degree of highness or lowness of a tone. It relates more to the quality of sound governed by the vibrations producing it. Volume is the loudness of sound. It has more to do with the amount of a sound. Tempo is the rate or speed of sound. It relates to number and duration of pauses in speaking. Thrust is the stress given on a syllable that renders it prominent within a word or a sentence. It relates to the meaning intended to be conveyed.

So how does knowledge of prosodic feature connect with the apt representation? Of course, you can't regulate them real-time. What is required is the cognizance of their importance and attention towards them. It charts the path to make subtle corrections that have huge impact. For example, if you are perceived as arrogant, sarcastic, mean, indifferent or disinterested then it is a classic case of your vocal cues superseding verbal cues. Spot what's amiss, and correct.

Mannerism relaxed:

The way one carries oneself has a great effect on the way they are treated by others. It is as if people sniff your self-image and then treat it as a reference-point to customize their behavior with you. What is colloquially called 'body language' has a lot to do with it. Taking a cue from the first point in this section, the pace of gestures has a bearing on the perceived status of the person. Relaxation in body language is an essential feature of dominance and superiority.

Slow and methodical movements are the hallmark of self-assured and in-control people. They seem to follow what Peter Collett calls 'principle of economy' whereas nervous and timid people seem to follow 'principle of effort'. As self-assured people are clear on their stance on a matter, their movements are smooth and unhurried. On the other hand, confused or non-committal people are unsure of themselves so they break into rapid and jerky movements.

Moreover, while self-assured people persist with a gesture, confused people keep changing their gestures all the time. This concept was beautifully explained by the great philosopher Nietzsche. When asked "what is aristocratic?" he replied "The slow gesture and the slow glance". Taking a leaf out of Nietzsche's book will lubricate your social interaction, and resultant smoothness of your portrayal and participation shall pave way for your 'apt representation'.

Expressions stable:

Nothing represents our emotions more clearly than our facial expressions. The reason is simple. While the gestures and postures can reveal our emotional state – positive or negative – the exact emotion that one is feeling can only be ascertained through one's facial expressions. They are real-time reflections of what we are feeling. That's why they are rapid, transient and ever-changing; and that's the base from which their role in 'apt representation' emerges.

People who are immature or amateur tend to wear their heart on their sleeves and content of it on their faces. That's why their faces are never short of expressions. In fact, the expressions are apparent, intense and fluctuating. They are sad at one moment, happy at another, and then suddenly they are toggling between the two. If you have such a face then, though you will come across as interesting and authentic, sadly you will be seen as unstable and fluctuating.

While this trait can be appreciated occasionally and partially in very close relationships, it is generally not considered apt for most of the relationships in your professional as well as personal domains. In fact, as an adult, it is important to learn to express your emotions without getting emotional. This way, you can convey feelings without overwhelming the other person and sabotaging your impression. In fact, this will help you in stabilizing your expressions.

Posture upright:

Posture is a relatively stationary body-position a person assumes. And how we hold our bodies tells a lot about us. It is representative of our moods, mental state and attitudes, and in many ways, it is a far reliable cue than brief gestures. There is a science to it – a 'foot to brain' connection. The feet are embedded with millions of fast acting touch receptors. So, as we stand or walk, these touch receptors in the feet are stimulated in certain patterns.

These patterns of stimulation (which are formed in the feet) send signals to the cerebellum (the balance center of the brain). The brain automatically responds to these signals by adjusting the body's posture according to the input it receives from the feet. Thus, a person's posture has a strong connection with what is going on in the brain. Hence we have many possible types of postures – upright, slumped, slouched, tensed, relaxed, leaning, withdrawing, aggressing etc.

Now, what we can call 'apt posture' will depend on situational factors. For instance, those who are judged as inattentive are the ones who don't subtly incline towards the speaker, or those who are considered as disinterested are the ones who sit in a slumped or slouched manner. So, some minor changes in posture can bring a difference. Having said that, in most situations, uprightness is one common ingredient in all the postures that are considered as appropriate.

Looking at listener(s):

The direction of gaze tells a lot about a person's mental state, and we humans are programmed to read it; more so because, while living in group, gauging what is drawing other person's attention and how it is affecting them had a direct bearing on one's own survival, because it gave a signal to base one's own responses on. And the most important straightforward principle is that we look at things that interest us and away from things that don't. Yes, 'direction' matters.

Another important expresser of eye-contact or gaze is 'duration'. Though 'acceptable duration' of a stare is more of a cultural issue, during a conversation, having an eye-contact for two-third of the duration is usually considered as normal. Stated in simple terms, duration of eye contact is proportional to the level of interest. That's why eye-contact usually increases significantly when we find something worth paying closer attention to.

Interestingly, often one thing feeds into another. We look more at people we like and we like people who look more at us. This point is of special significance in terms of 'apt representation'. Whether as speaker or listener, it is important to maintain a humble eye-contact with the other person. If there are multiple then it is crucial to divide your attention wisely to make all of them feel acknowledged. Absence of doing so runs a risk of being misinterpreted as uninterested.

Approach frontal:

The importance of the orientation of our torso in the domain of nonverbal behavior has roots in our evolutionary past. The frontal part of our body has most of the organs vital for our survival, and damage to any of them could be fatal. Thus when a human being was threatened by some predator or enemy, first reaction was to hide, turn away or cover the frontal portion or head. Even today, though for contextually different reasons, in aforementioned feelings, we behave same.

Thus we choose ventral fronting towards what we like and resort to ventral denial for things we don't like. That's why you find people bent forward and hanging onto each word of a likeable speaker, and turned away, deep in their seats, if speaker is unlikeable. Similar cues can be seen when people greet and meet each other with open arms if there is trust and liking, culminating often into a hug. On the other hand, folding arms or angling away is natural in case of repulsion.

In terms of 'apt representation', except when situational factors demand otherwise, it is good to generally keep a frontal approach. It is indicative of receptiveness towards ideas, openness towards propositions, affinity towards the other person, agreeableness in face of conflict, flexibility in temperament, and overall likeability. Often, when people are generally seen as opposite to the aforesaid, one of the contributing factors is the approach of their torso.

Nodding natural:

Head-movements communicate a great deal, telling a lot about two points – rapport and interest. They get manifested by two things: whether the head is moving or is still, and whether the movement is horizontal or vertical. If head is still then it conveys that either the person hasn't understood the point or dislikes the point or 'you'. Thus, head movement represents synchrony that people have. That's why, when we nod, we expect other person to nod back.

Nodding vertically is a universal gesture for receptiveness and agreement. Generally, a slow, lengthy and rhythmic vertical-nodding shows that the listener is following the point, and wishes you to carry on. As a close variant, small nods, if accompanied with a smile, convey that the listener is not only interested in your point but also finds you likeable and 'worthy of pleasing'. On the contrary, in most cultures, horizontal nodding signifies connotations of disagreement.

In terms of 'apt representation', nodding plays an important role in the sense that it primes the other person to infer your stand as well as stance. If you are nodding aptly in a conversation, you are seen as sensible, present, invested and affable. A stiff head at the time of greeting or in the course of a conversation positions you as a difficult, arrogant or disinterested person. So, you see, just a small conscious change can work wonders in being seen in the positive light.

The use of 'space' in communication is of such importance that there is a whole branch of study devoted to it - Proxemics. Like most animals, human beings express territorial behavior, which means, they stake out a claim to a physical space or entity that they believe belongs to them. In civilized social settings, hands and arms are important means to express this sense of territoriality. They are constantly used to mark territories.

A dominating person would usually spread arms horizontally to claim a larger space. Sitting on a sofa or bench, they would cover the whole three-seater by spreading their arms along the topside/backside of the sofa. Even sitting on a chair, their arm may spread up to the chair next to theirs. Many gestures have come out of this tendency to claim a larger space – like standing in an akimbo position or sitting with legs in a figure-four position.

On the other hand, people tend to almost shrink themselves when they are feeling nervous, afraid or conscious. While sitting or standing, they cover lesser space than their body naturally occupies. They also use arms or hands to cover their body. In terms of 'apt representation', either extreme is inadvisable. It is always preferred to occupy the natural body-space and thus come across as someone who is 'confident and assertive' yet 'agreeable and receptive'.

10

The 'Self Awareness' Skill-Pill

What is it about?

You will come across this term in all forms of literature; whether it belongs to spirituality, psychology, philosophy, religion or even neuroscience. What makes 'self awareness' such a sought after term? Well, it is the fact that it is the underlying 'first step' towards any form of intrapersonal or interpersonal intervention. Everything begins here. After all, how can one do something about what is going on around them without knowing what is going on inside them!

It has two major facets – introspection and retrospection. To introspect is to look inwards and to retrospect is to look backwards. While former helps you identify complexes, insecurities, biases and agendas that have been a constant companion in your life journey, latter helps you in seeing the potholes that impacted the tires of the vehicle of your mind vis-à-vis the roads you travelled. The content that comes out as a result of the two is then worthy of being processed.

When it comes to people with intrapersonal and interpersonal issues, lack of self-awareness is a common challenge. They have either not taken stock of emotional inventory or have never paid heed to processing emotions properly. Forget about hygiene and catharsis, many have not even taken out time to identify or address their emotions. In other words, there is a black-box that they have chosen to treat as a blind spot. A potent prevention to this is the skill-pill – **SelAwa.**

What are its ingredients?

SWAGGER they are:

S – Shame

W – Worry

A – Angst

G – Guilt

G – Grief

E – Envy

R – Remorse

Why and how do its ingredients work?

Shame:

In many cases, at the root of one's emotional and behavioral issues lies a hidden shy emotion – shame. But to do something about it, one has to spot it first. So let's understand what are its features and factors. Shame is essentially an emotion felt vis-à-vis others, and involves a sense of being exposed and suddenly becoming subject to others' judgment. You feel as if something embarrassing, inappropriate or flawed about you has become evident to others.

Shame is accompanied by a sudden spike in self-consciousness. You become acutely aware of yourself. You feel a sense of aloneness and 'sticking out' in contrast of surroundings. It renders you lonely as you have to bear it all by yourself. It forces you into hiding. You feel like running away, far from those who just got to know 'that which cannot be named'. And as Dr. Salman Akhtar says "there is an imaginary glance directed at you, and you feel like covering your face".

This desire to hide can be related to one's physical attributes (like pimple, specs or braces) or bodily functions (like farting or belching) or possessions (dress, car or house). The criterion is simple – you do not want anyone to see them. Among other factors, three responses by your primary caregivers in formative years play a role behind it – exasperation on your small failures, exaggerated reaction on your minor achievements, and mocking of a bodily feature of yours.

Worry:

You feel nervous and irritable. You are hopelessly preoccupied with a particular thread of thoughts. You feel physically restless and find it difficult to be at ease. You can't sit peacefully and keep pacing around. Your appetite goes down and you find it difficult to fall asleep. Well, that's 'worry' for you. It is an unpleasant emotional state that takes complete hold of you (the word is actually derived from the German word 'wurgen' which means 'to strangle')

Well, worry is essentially the cognitive counterpart of 'anxiety'. It is born out of a concern for something that is either impending or anticipated. Thus, it has a 'what-if' component. You create scenarios in your head which are built around the loss of something valuable. While a healthy extent of doing so can help one become proactive, leading to better preparation and preparedness; in worry, our predicting-machine called 'mind' goes into an overdrive.

In this regard, it is important to understand that 'what one worries about' provides valuable information about their psychological needs. Some worry about loss of money, some about loss of health, some about loss of dear ones, some about loss of repute and then some about loss of opportunity. What's peculiar is that each category finds other category's reason for worry not worthy enough. An analysis of 'why it is so' can reveal a lot about what's going on subliminally.

Angst:

Angst is a strange emotion. In fact, it is better to call it an emotional state – a state in which you feel anxiety mixed with negativity and frustration. It doesn't make you restless like the worry does. It rather leaves you with a sense of displeasure, unease and dissatisfaction simmering on the backburner. It need not be about something specific, it can be about the general state of affairs in life or world. It also carries components of cynicism, disillusionment and rebellion.

A well-known form of angst is what is called 'existential angst'. Well, an intrinsic human need is to give a meaning to one's existence (who am I, and what am I here for). This meaningfulness is a prerequisite for maintaining mental health. It keeps you anchored and sane. The best part is that the answer to this question need not be profound or eternal. What matters is that you have an answer that can help you navigate your actions and choices through an inner compass.

This answer helps you develop internal resources to exercise your free will for unleashing your unique set of abilities and skills. On the other hand, its absence leaves you purposeless, lost and generally irritable for no reasons. This doesn't happen to all people with equal intensity. Those who are highly sensitive are more prone to feel angst and thus have a more pressing need to find practicable answers to existential, fundamental or philosophical questions of life and work.

Guilt:

Guilt is a higher order emotion. While you would find the basic universal emotions like sadness, fear and anger becoming apparent right from childhood, you would rarely find anyone feeling guilty before they have reached a certain age. The reason is simple – it is felt in reference to an established 'moral or social' norm (ethics or laws). That's why, only after someone has gone through enough conditioning or acculturation, they are prone to experiencing guilt.

Just like shame, guilt is an aversive (the difference is that, while in shame, you feel like hiding, in guilt, you feel like confessing) self-conscious emotion which is triggered due to one of the four reasons – wrong actions committed by you, assumed wrong actions committed by you, right actions you did not commit, and imagined wrong actions (even thoughts). Thus, it is a socially utile emotion coming from 'good governance' instilled in us to align with pro-social behavior.

Guilt is an active emotion – it gets us to act. So the best way to deal with guilt is to do something about it – apologize, amend or atone. That's why the most painful form of guilt to address is the one that you feel towards someone who is gone – out of reach, or dead. This is what bothers most people with emotional problems. It requires a reassessment of one's behavior, a reframing of one's attitude towards it, or a 'replacement act' as atonement.

Grief:

There is a difference between sadness and grief. While sadness lowers your energy and breeds inertia, grieving mobilizes your energy towards an action (like weeping). Grieving takes place in wake of a loss. While the term is generally used in context of loss of a loved one, broadly speaking, it can also include loss of a valued material possession, a cherished relationship, or even an important part of one's life (like an entrepreneurial venture shutting down).

Usually, grieving follows a natural course. It starts with disbelief and then is replaced by a spike of emotional pain. It is then followed by a sense of longing. After some time, idealization and then regretting over 'what could have been done to prevent the loss' follow. Phases of blaming oneself and feeling anguish also come. The bereaved fluctuates between loneliness, sadness, heartache and resigned acceptance. Eventually, one starts to cope with it and adapt ahead.

An incomplete grieving can manifest in the form of debilitating symptoms. One may become inert in one's life, or experience inexplicable anxiety, or feel emotional flattening, or become a workaholic, or witness a change in mentality (pessimism or cynicism), or feel a need for social withdrawal, or experience an unusually strong pull towards religiosity, spirituality, astrology or occult. Only a process of going back and freeing the stuck lever in mind can do the needful.

**Envy:**

Envy is a peculiarly unpleasant feeling that you have when you realize that someone else has what you desire or deserve (probably 'more' than the other person). So, one can feel envious towards someone's physical attributes, social resourcefulness, material assets, state of affairs, mental faculties, creative abilities, and even emotional serenity or spiritual progression. You want it for yourself, and the fact that you can't have it right away makes you feel terrible.

Having said that, a little envy is not that bad, as it mobilizes your effort towards emulating the other person's best practices to get closer to the envied object or trait. However, higher degree of it leaves you with such a bitter taste in mouth that you feel inferior, dejected, and at times even paralyzed in your effort. There is a thorn that manifests as a scorn and you even withdraw yourself from such people, and to feel good, instead surround yourself with lesser people.

At the base of it, too much envy is born out of desperation to be accepted and appreciated. In many cases, the cause of it dates back to the lack of consistent availability and love of parental figures (especially mother) in early childhood, and the anguish born out of this kind of internal deprivation later manifests as envy. If that deprivation gets filled up by authentic acceptance, the anguish decreases, and the envy becomes manageably tolerable.

Remorse is a burdensome feeling. It is different from the guilt in a sense that while guilt arises from having impulses to commit acts that are prohibited by ethics or laws, remorse is a dark uneasy feeling arising from the awareness of having done something hurtful to someone close. So while guilt is prominently about impulses, remorse is about actual action. Moreover, while regret is self-directed, in remorse, one is mindful of the hurt/harm of one's actions upon others.

So it can result from abandoning someone in times of need, or doing a volte-face on a promise that someone based their choices upon, or failing to acknowledge a dear one's legitimate need. There is no easy remedy for remorse and in fact any attempt to resolve remorse superficially only makes the matter worse. It starts with a genuine heartfelt self-admission that one has indeed done something hurtful. It has to be followed by sincere apology and compensatory act.

However, a 'too quick' compensation without the preceding steps can aggravate the trauma of the hurt. Moreover, your unaddressed remorse can cause to you a great damage in the form of pinch of the conscience and lower self-esteem. If it stays for long, it can lead to self-destructive tendencies like excessive addiction or even self-harm behavior. In all, one's redemption takes a slow and steady process marked by clear milestones not to be skipped or taken casually.